ther na

anner

can scar
pictures
compu
scanner
mage of
re you p
great too
own art
es.

Items must be returned on or before the last date
stamped below, or overdue charges will be made.

D1313437

4/08

11/2

1 3 MAY 2009

2 8 APR 2010

LIB (a)

Written by Liz Pratt
Illustrated by Ian Cunliffe

Published by Ladybird Books Ltd
A Penguin Company
Penguin Books Ltd, 80 Strand, London WC2R 0RL, UK
Penguin Books Australia Ltd, Camberwell, Victoria, Australia
Penguin Books (NZ) Ltd, 67 Apollo Drive, Mairangi Bay, Auckland, New Zealand

3 5 7 9 10 8 6 4 2

ISBN-13: 978-1-84422-623-8
ISBN-10: 1-8442-2623-9

Printed in Italy

Computers
for
School

Computers are EVERYWHERE!

There are lots of computers we never see, but they still affect our lives.

Traffic lights

Pedestrian crossings and traffic lights are controlled by computers.

Mobile phones

Mobile phones are controlled by a system run by computers. Some phones today can access the Internet and send and receive e-mail.

Supermarkets

Ever wondered why the groceries 'bleep' when the checkout operator pushes them along the conveyor belt? A computer is reading a series of lines known as the barcode. This then tells the computer in the till how much everything costs.

Give it a try

Try counting how many seconds it takes for the traffic lights to change colour next time a car is stopped by them. The timing is controlled by a computer.

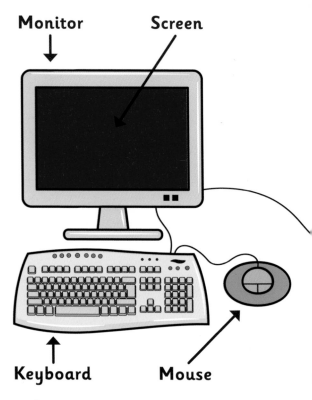

Monitor   **Screen**

Keyboard   **Mouse**

The tower houses the CPU, memory and hard disk drives, where you can store all the information you need.

It helps to know the names of all the different parts to your computer so that you can follow instructions easily.

Tower

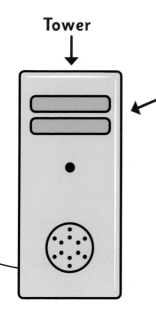

Disk drives

If we take a closer look at the computer we can see the DISK DRIVES.

Can you locate a floppy disk drive, a CD ROM/ DVD drive, or a CD Rewriter (CDRW) on your computer?

On a LAPTOP computer, the CPU and the MONITOR are all part of the same unit.

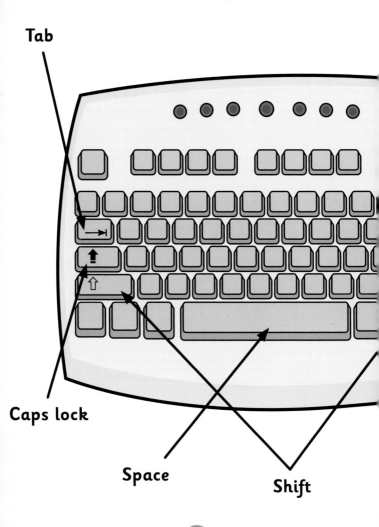

Tab

Caps lock

Space

Shift

The keys on a computer have different jobs. Getting to know the keyboard helps you to work more quickly.

Delete

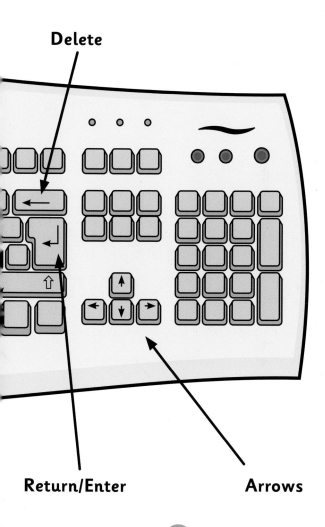

Return/Enter

Arrows

11

Some important keys

Q W E Letter keys

Most keyboards have letter keys shown in UPPER CASE (capitals) although sometimes children's keyboards are shown in lower case (small letters)

⇧ Shift

This changes the text to upper case. It is useful when you only have one or two capital letters to type, like at the beginning of your name. You must keep it pressed down while you are typing.

⬆ Caps lock

This changes the letters from lower case to upper case, and the other way around. IT IS USEFUL IF YOU HAVE A LOT OF WORDS IN CAPITAL LETTERS, LIKE THIS.

Space

This makes a short break between one word and the next.

These are keys that you are likely to use a lot. Getting to know them well will make it easy to use a keyboard.

 Return

When you are writing on the computer, use this key to create space between paragraphs. On some programs you press this when you want to move to the next screen.

 Tab

This moves the cursor across the screen in big jumps so that you can type further along the line.

 Direction arrows

These move the cursor quickly around the screen: up, down, and across.

 Delete

Use this to get rid of type when you have made a mistake or changed your mind.

Microphone

You can attach a microphone to your computer to record and add sound files to your stories and pictures.

Web cam

This is a small video camera that transmits through your computer. This camera can send moving sound and pictures across the Internet. You could talk to a relative in Australia and watch them make funny faces at you if you both have web cams.

Scanner

You can scan documents and pictures directly into your computer. The scanner will scan an image of the text or picture you place on it. This is a great tool for inserting your own artwork into your stories.

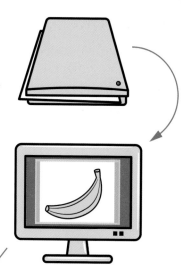

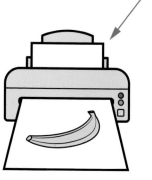

Printer

All good artists and authors want to see their work published on paper. Your printer can help you to do this. It will print in full colour or in black and white if you ask it to.

Starting to type

First, go to a word processing program.

Then create a NEW DOCUMENT.

Then you are ready to type.

When you have typed what you want to, look at some of the other menus at the top of the screen.

The EDIT menu helps you to change the order of what you have written:

Highlight the words you want to move by holding down the button on your mouse.

Click CUT on the edit menu.

Move the cursor to where you want the words to be.

Click on PASTE. The words will appear in the new position. You can change the order of the text until you are happy.

You can type anything you like! Emails, letters, posters or notices.

You can also try changing how your text is laid out.

Find the place on your screen that helps you to CENTRE text. Like this.

Find out how to make your text appear on the RIGHT margin of the page. Like this.

Make sure when you sit at a computer that your hands and wrists are comfortable and you are not reaching over anything to type.

Fun with fonts!

These are some other things you can do to change what you have written.

Some fonts are designed to make things look handwritten

like this...

Some fonts are used because they are easy to read

like this

Some fonts are used simply because they look good.

like this or **this one**

Give it a try

Type the name of your school into your computer. Now change the font until YOU think it looks good.

Try to make it look serious, playful, fun, or welcoming.

The font is the *style* of the print.
Experimenting with fonts is great fun.

To change the font on anything you have typed into a document you must first SELECT your text by clicking and dragging over the words you wish to change, to highlight them.

Now you can change the font to suit the work you are doing.

Over to you

Which font would you choose for:
- party invitations
- a letter to your teacher
- a greeting card to an older friend or relative
- a sign for your bedroom door

Where will I get my pictures?

- You can use the CLIPART already in your computer.
- You can DOWNLOAD an image from the Internet.
- You can take a digital photograph.
- You can draw and save your own picture in a paint package.
- You can use a scanner to scan one of your own masterpieces into the computer.

All of the saved pictures (images) will be stored in files somewhere in your computer's memory.

When you want to include them in your work you will need to find the "INSERT" tool on your computer program.

Then you will have to find where you have stored your saved picture before you can insert it into your work.

Pictures make your work more colourful and pleasing to look at. Even better if the picture is one of your own!

Give it a try

Make a door plate for your friend's bedroom and include a piece of clipart that reminds you of them.

Write a postcard from your dream holiday and illustrate it with a picture downloaded from the internet.

Make a scrapbook of your digital photographs by writing a sentence to go beneath each image telling the viewer all about it.

Resize and make miniature copies of your own works of art to make into bookmarks to give as gifts.

All of the work you create and save on your computer is stored in FILES in your computer's memory.

To help to organise everything in your computer, files are stored in FOLDERS.

The first time you want to save a piece of work, a 'save as' box will appear. You must decide where (in which folder) to save your work, and what you will call it.

If you want to take these files away from the computer you are working on, you can save them onto a floppy disk, a CD or a memory stick. Saving your work like this means that you can view and continue your work on another computer.

You don't have to finish your work all in one go, you can save it and come back to it later.

Opening saved work

Before you can open a saved piece of work, you have to remember where you saved it! Go to the folder or disk where it was saved and double click on the file you want to open. Your computer will automatically open that file in the program that was used to create it.

If you can't remember where you put your file, ask your computer via the 'search' or 'find' item on the menu.

The 'save' button will automatically save any work using the last name the file was given. It will OVERWRITE your last work on the same file.

The Internet and World Wide Web

Where can you see what the astronauts in space see from the window of their spaceship, write your name in hieroglyphics, sing the lyrics to your favourite song or see what it's like to stand on the top of the highest mountain?

The Internet, of course!

Although the Internet is a wonderful place to play, to work and to collect information, before you use it you must always ask permission from an adult.

The World Wide Web is part of the Internet. It is an enormous and wonderful source of information to those who use it correctly.

How to find a website

All websites have an 'address'. To find a particular website, type the web address into the bar of your web browser and click on 'go'.

If you don't know the exact address of the website that you want, try using a 'search engine'. Ask a teacher to find out how to do this.

Give it a try

Type www.ladybird.co.uk into your Internet address bar to look at the activities on offer at Ladybird.

Rules to remember:

You must never give out your personal details; full name, address, telephone number, or photograph over the Internet.

Kids and parents can find out more about surfing safely at:

www.kidsmart.org.uk

Use fonts and colours to make calligrams (words that look like their meaning).

Making changes

Write your own version of a traditional fairy story. Save your work. When you come back to your computer, open the story and re-write the ending. You could make it as funny as you like.

Internet treasure

If you could travel back in time, where would you go? To the pyramids of Egypt, the first Olympic Games in Ancient Greece or to the days of travel and adventure in Tudor times?

Use a children's search engine to find out more about these times to help you make your decision.

www.ajkids.com
www.yahooligans.com

Test your spelling

Choose some words you find difficult to spell. Type them into a word processing program and use the spell check to correct any mistakes. Keep practising until you get them right first time.

Make an activities timetable

What do you do with your time outside school? Make a chart for each day of the week and insert clipart to show you how to fill your time. If you go swimming on Monday, choose a swimmer to insert next to Monday and so on…

Useful vocabulary

CD

This stands for 'Compact Disk'. We use these for storing big files or lots of information.

CPU

Central Processing Unit - this is where your computer does all of its "thinking".

Cut

The item on the 'edit' menu that enables you to take a block of words away from one place.

Desktop

When you open your computer the first screen it stops at is your desktop. This is the place where your program icons are and where you begin your work.

Document

A file that looks like a sheet of paper on your screen. You can type onto a document.

There are lots of words you need to know when you work with a computer. Here are just a few to get you started.

Download   Transferring files or information from the Internet onto an individual computer.

Floppy disk   These disks are used for storing small files. They don't look floppy at all on the outside but are certainly floppy on the inside!

Hardware   All the bits of your computer, monitor, keyboard, printer etc.

Icons   Icons are small pictures or symbols to help you to find the program or action you are looking for.

Internet   An enormous network of information accessed through the World Wide Web.

Intranet

A mini private version of the Internet which allows only the people in the school or company to view the websites on offer.

Monitor

The monitor is the screen where you view your work.

Mouse

A pointing, selecting, drawing and dragging tool. These are usually found in standard roller-ball (with a ball underneath to track its movement across the mouse mat) or optical (with a light sensor underneath to track movement over any surface).

Overwrite

Making changes to a document that has already been saved as something different.